DROITWICH
A Pictorial History

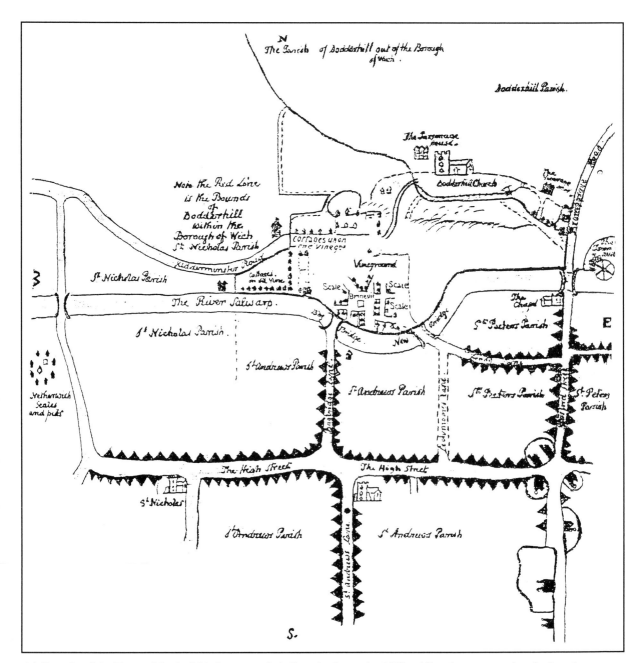

'A Draught of the Town of Droitwich'. Some people believe its date to be 1640, while others suspect it to be later because of the shape of Dodderhill church, which was rebuilt in 1708.

DROITWICH
A Pictorial History

Lyn Blewitt & Bob Field

Phillimore

1994

Published by
PHILLIMORE & CO. LTD.,
Shopwyke Manor Barn, Chichester, West Sussex

ISBN 0 85033 902 2

Printed and bound in Great Britain by
BIDDLES LTD.
Guildford, Surrey

List of Illustrations

Frontispiece: 17th-century map

The authors' proceeds from the sale of this book will go to the Droitwich History and Archaeology Society and the Droitwich Brine Springs & Archaeological Trust

DROITWICH HISTORY AND ARCHAEOLOGY SOCIETY began in 1984 with the aims of providing a focus for local interest in Droitwich's heritage, educating individuals and organisations about what remains, promoting awareness of possible conservation measures, and expanding current knowledge levels by practical work. Monthly lectures are held, visits arranged, newsletters produced and projects undertaken. Long-term commitments include a study of Salwarpe parish and participation in the 1881 Census Project, while collaboration with Droitwich Spa Civic Society resulted in Audits of Archaeology, and of Conservation and Listed Buildings, in Droitwich. The publication of *Droitwich: A Pictorial History* is part of the Society's tenth anniversary celebrations.

LYN BLEWITT AND BOB FIELD

DROITWICH BRINE SPRINGS & ARCHAEOLOGICAL TRUST began as a registered charity in 1987, its purpose to advance understanding of the ancient salt industry, its technology, archaeology and history. It is the aim of the Trust to establish a permanent museum at the site of the Upwich Pit, in Vines Park in order to promote and join in promoting public education, restoration and conservation of this historical site. Its purpose to advance and assist studies and research into the geology and natural history of this preservation area as a site of special scientific interest. At an earlier time, in the 1950s, Mrs. Beatrice Hopkinson and her husband Julian, as STUDIO BIJOU, made a collection and recorded a pictorial history of the changing face of Droitwich. Part of this collection is now loaned for publication to benefit both the Droitwich Brine Springs and Archaeological Trust, and the Droitwich History and Archaeology Society; they are numbered as follows in the List of Illustrations overleaf: 3-6, 8, 11, 13-16, 18-20, 23, 26, 28, 39, 42-44, 46-53, 55-59, 61-62, 71-72, 74, 76-77, 79-80, 83-88, 90-94, 104-107, 109-111, 115-118, 122, 124, 126-132, 134, 137-139, 141-142, 145, 147-149, 151-154, 156, 160, 162, 164-168.

BEATRICE HOPKINSON

Acknowledgements

The authors would like to thank the following for their help in producing this book. For the text, the Hereford and Worcester County Archaeological Service and particularly Mr. Derek Hurst and Mr. Simon Woodiwiss, former Droitwich Archaeological Officers; Droitwich Town Council and its Town Clerk, Mr. Graham Pharo; and Mr. Chris Pancheri. For the photographs and captions, the County Record Office staff and the County Archivist, Mr. Tony Wherry; and Mr. Clive Haines. We also would like to thank the various copyright holders for the use of the photographs: Mrs. A. Horsley, Mr. J. Potter, Mr. D. J. Wills, Mrs. Hodgkinson, Mr. A. G. Jension RIBA, Mr. A. Mapletoft, Miss L. Baker, Mr. G. H. Haycox, Mr. R. F. Cotton, Mr. A. J. Woodley, Mr. T. Lewis, Mr. G. B. Bate, Dr. T. M. Galloway, Mr. D. P. Verge, Mr. E. Taylor, Mr. E. H. Sergeant, Mr. P. G. Matthews, Mr. W. T. Jones, Mr. A. C. Derrick, Mr. K. C. Adkins, Mr. R. Fleetwood and Mr. Paviour.

Introduction

It is impossible to cover adequately the rich history and heritage of Droitwich in a brief introduction, so this is a short account of the salt industry followed by what is known now (or can be supposed on reasonable grounds) about the growth and development of the town. On that subject, the reader should be aware that until the late 18th century the course of the River Salwarpe was not as at present; the map (frontispiece) shows the topography of the Salwarpe and of the town as it was for most of Droitwich's history.

The Salt Industry

Brine streams 200 ft. below ground are forced to the surface in what is now the Vines Park area of the Salwarpe valley; at 25 per cent salt, this brine is very strong (seawater is three per cent salt; Droitwich brine is saltier than the Dead Sea!) and is thus a natural resource of great value throughout history.

In the Palaeolithic Age (40,000 B.C.) herbivorous animals were attracted to the brackish brine pools; human activity in this area dates from Mesolithic times (8000-4000 B.C.), when hunters may have waited for their prey at the briny marshes. Neolithic (4000-2000 B.C.) or Bronze Age (2000-800 B.C.) worked flints from Droitwich indicate human activity at this time.

In the Iron Age (800 B.C.-A.D. 43), and in particular during the third and second centuries B.C., a well-organised, large-scale salt industry was established to the south of the Salwarpe (Friar Street area), and there is also evidence for production at Bays Meadow, Upwich and Dodderhill. The method used was evaporation of the brine over fires to produce salt crystals, which were raked off and put into containers to dry out, and then transported. This method continued throughout the two thousand years of the salt industry. Iron Age people constructed large tanks in the ground, which they lined with wood and clay; brine was collected in these tanks, probably left for the impurities to settle to the bottom, and then boiled over hearths. The crystals were packed into coarse clay pots (*briquetage*), in which the dried salt was also transported over a wide area to the west, south and east. This activity was seasonal in later times, and may also have been in its early stages; if so, the Iron-Age salt-workers may not have lived permanently in the immediate area. The industry at this time generated great wealth for its owners or controllers; gold coins were found in Droitwich and at Hanbury.

The Romans (A.D. 43-410), even before their invasion of Britain, would have been aware of the Droitwich salt industry and its wealth, and indeed a fort was built here almost immediately after the frontier had been pushed westward to the Severn. A more permanent fort on Dodderhill existed from A.D. 60 to A.D. 100, indicating military control of the industry—salt production throughout the Roman world was under direct imperial control—and Roman roads radiated out from the town. On the major Iron-Age site, the old production methods continued into the second century. A geographical book of A.D. 140-50 records a 'Salinae' (salt springs) which is almost certainly Droitwich; during the second century, major engineering works around the main brine springs (later Upwich, in Vines Park) indicate a huge crane or winch, and it is possible that the 'great well' referred to in Saxon charters was built by the Romans at this time. Control of the industry from about A.D. 150 was probably exercised by a civilian administrator, who lived in the villa built on Bays Meadow.

Following the Roman withdrawal from Britain, little is known for sure about events, either from documentary or archaeological sources, during the Dark Ages (the sub-Roman and early Anglo-Saxon centuries). In Droitwich, as the importance of salt was so great, it seems certain that the industry continued; following the Anglo-Saxons' arrival in the Severn valley (A.D. 577), and possibly before that, stone-lined channels supporting lead pans were constructed on top of the Roman features at the main brine springs; these open-air brine hearths were sheltered by wattle windbreaks, so that the temperature of the fire could be controlled to avoid melting the lead! Pottery finds indicate salt trading with other areas in this early Saxon period. Following major flooding of the Salwarpe, the riverbank was reinforced in the seventh or eighth centuries and widespread trading continued. Several documents from this time describe or refer to Droitwich, including a large number of Saxon charters; its name then was 'Wic' or 'Saltwic', and by the 10th century the three main brine wells of Upwich (the 'great well'), Middlewich and Netherwich appear in the charters. Royal interest and ownership is indicated, and the Mercian royal family had a 'royal vill' or hall (palace, possibly) at Wychbold; their ownership of the salt and its wealth may well have been a factor in that kingdom's rise to eminence. By the end of the Saxon era, pottery in Droitwich indicates trading links with Lincolnshire, Bedfordshire, Oxfordshire and probably Staffordshire.

The Norman Conquest was followed by the survey known as Domesday Book, which shows that royal ownership of the salt continued: 'Wych' produced 1,000 tons of salt a year, and is valued at about £90, three times as much as Worcester! Production methods and transportation of the salt probably continued as before; production was of course dependent on the supply of wood for fuel, and there are entries in both Saxon charters and Domesday Book which suggest that, increasingly, this had to be brought in from some distance away.

In 1215 King John's charter granted to the burgesses of Droitwich all the king's rights over salt production, in exchange for an annual rent of £100 (the same as for Newcastle-upon-Tyne, a great trading port). The industry was organised and profits were made locally, but in 1264-5 the Great Pit (of Roman or Saxon date) had to be rebuilt as the brine supply failed due to the pit's dilapidated condition. This was a massive engineering feat, given the waterlogged conditions; the new pit was 10 ft. square and 30 ft. deep, made of oak beams overlapped at the corners and caulked with moss. A ladder fixed to the inside enabled the pit to be maintained, and a beam above the pit supported the 'common bucket' which, guided by ropes, brought the brine from the pit to be poured into barrels set into the ground. After settling, the brine was taken to boiling houses nearby to be evaporated in three-feet-square lead pans over hearths, and the salt crystals were packed into conical wicker baskets. The town benefited from the wealth of the industry, and an Exchequer House was built in which the burgesses met to govern the industry; but the ownership of salt rights and burgess-ship was jealously restricted during the town's monopoly. The name 'Dryghtwych', meaning either 'princely/lordly' or 'dirty' 'wych', first appears in the 14th century. Production was seasonal, between June and December; a few extra weeks were worked at the end of this time, and total production would have been around 1,500 tons by the 15th century, when a pump was constructed at the Upwich pit, using hollowed elm trunks. Six thousand cartloads of wood were consumed each salt-making season (six months), resulting in heavy air pollution in the Salwarpe valley and town.

During the 16th and 17th centuries the introduction of iron pans and coal as a fuel enabled output to increase to 3,000 tons a year; brick flues were tried out from 1678. Six types of salt were being made, with some exported to the west country and to Ireland. The monopoly was still very much in force, though, with production restricted to the brine from the main pits.

In 1695 Robert Steynor won a court case which broke the monopoly, and from then on new brine wells were sunk by inhabitants who did not contribute to the annual rent; production increased, the price of salt declined gradually, and the old social order in the town changed rapidly. New technology such as brick-lined, deeper brine wells and steam engines for pumping meant a rapid increase in production during the 18th century, with salt being made throughout the year; by 1772, 15,000 tons were made each year. The old pits, still burdened with the Crown's annual rent, became uneconomic; Upwich was out of use by 1737.

The Droitwich Barge Canal was constructed 1768-71 to transport salt to the Severn at Hawford, and to bring in coal. During the 19th century large factories were built in the Vines and Covercroft areas, using iron pans 23 ft. by 13 ft. over multiple brick flues; brine was piped in to these factories from open brick reservoirs which were supplied from brine wells 80-100 ft. deep, from which hollow copper rods went down a further 100 ft. to tap the underground brine streams. The railway arrived in 1852, when the canal was extended to the east to meet the Worcester and Birmingham Canal at Hanbury Wharf. Production peaked in 1872 at 120,000 tons, but from 1892 the industry was transferred to the newer works at Stoke Prior, and in 1922 the last salt works in Droitwich closed down.

Development of the Town

Iron Age

Little is known about dwellings or other structures connected with the salt industry at this time; round-houses existed at Bays Meadow, with a hearth for salt-making. This may have been a seasonal activity, with people coming in from habitation centres nearby. Iron-Age field systems are cut by one of the Roman roads (Worcester to Bromsgrove), and The Holloway and Newland Road may derive from pre-Roman trackways.

Roman

The fort on Dodderhill was in use from A.D. 60-100 only, and some of the timbers may have been re-used at the main brine well (later Upwich). Roman Salinae was a *vicus*, an industrial settlement rather than a town, thus lacking defences, public buildings, and a laid-out street plan. The salt industry was regulated and concentrated in the Vines Park area during the second century, when control was probably exercised by a civilian administrator living in the rich villa built on Bays Meadow. Surviving from the mid-second century to about A.D. 300, this complex had two main buildings, the larger with 18 rooms, underfloor central heating, mosaic floors, painted plaster walls, and rich furnishings. After the complex was burned *c*.A.D. 300, a barn was refurbished and extended, and occupied into the fifth century.

The commercial centre appears to have been at the Queen Street and Hanbury Street junction of two Roman roads. Further to the west, along Vines Lane (probably the line of the lost Roman road to the west), lay the cemetery which would have been outside the settlement. At the west end of Friar Street domestic occupation occurs until A.D. 200; between Friar Street and the river, salt production continued using Iron-Age methods into the second century, when a building was constructed; in about the fourth century a large timber-framed building on padstones went up on this site; the posts possibly survived into the 12th century. This was probably used for tanning or meat processing, activities often associated with the availability of brine or salt. Scatters of Romano-British pottery at Westwood Park and near Salwarpe suggest that the surrounding areas were being farmed.

Anglo-Saxon

At Upwich, new furnaces from the sixth (or possibly the fifth) century suggest the continuation of the salt industry, and of any settlement in the town area, through Romano-British and early Saxon times. Again, little evidence exists for the nature of the settlement; the west end of Friar Street shows agricultural use in the fifth century, with a possible small farmstead enclosure to the south. By the late Saxon era, this area was the site of a tannery, suggesting that it was at the edge of the settlement. At the east end of Friar Street, there is an indication of a late Saxon road to the north of the present street. (The large building erected in late Roman times remained in some form through this period also.) High Street is likely to be the earliest of the town centre streets, leading off the Roman road junction (Queen Street/Hanbury Street).

Droitwich's name at this time, 'wic', indicates that it was a commercial centre, as does the term *emptorio* used in eighth-century charters. The administrative centre for the area would have been the Mercian royal hall at Wychbold; Witton ('Wic-tun', farm by 'wic') was the agricultural settlement. So, this was an industrial and commercial centre, which in late Saxon times was moving towards town or borough status, even having a mint in the 11th century.

The Medieval Period and the Salt Monopoly

The Domesday Survey of 1086 indicates the size and economic importance of Droitwich (125 burgesses and 35 houses, four saltworkers and seven villeins; worth about £90 a year), and the royal ownership of salt production, but it is not named as a borough. This status is confirmed in 1155-6 records, and consolidated by King John's charter of 1215. As well as granting the salt industry to the borough, a weekly market and fair was granted, with the right to hold a borough court. Burgage plots are found in High Street, Queen Street and Friar Street; Tower Hill was the back lane for High Street. These plots are wide and not very deep, in line with other Midland towns of pre-Conquest origin; a similar date is indicated by the lack of room in the town layout for the market granted in the charter. There are two possible sites for this, the older probably the meeting place of High Street, Friar Street and St Andrew's Street, site of the Exchequer House; the other site is Queen Street, at the junction of Worcester Road and Hanbury Street.

The charter meant that townspeople could share in the wealth of the salt industry. The burgesses organised the industry, and the first Exchequer House was probably built soon after the charter. Following the failure and rebuilding in 1264-5 of the Great Pit, a fire starting in St Andrew's church destroyed much of the town in 1290; a new Exchequer House was built by 1327. (The site of this building, which was rebuilt in 1581 and survived until 1825, is not the present Town Hall site; instead, the Exchequer House was in the middle of the triangle, directly to the north of St Andrew's church, as stated in the description by Dr. Prattinton who visited it just before demolition. In 1628 a row of seven butchers' arches was added to its east end, where the stocks, pillory and pump were located; it would be impossible to extend in this way a building on the Town Hall site.)

The first recorded grant of *pavage* occurs in 1316 and *pontage* in 1331; these were royal licences allowing the burgesses to raise money by taxing certain goods, towards the cost of paving the streets and building or maintaining bridges. Droitwich was not enclosed by walls; instead a ditch was used to control access, with tollgates, one of which was at the east end of High Street and another at the south end of St Andrew's Street ('Worcester gate', mentioned in 1622). Most streets are recorded by the 14th century, including High Street, Friar Street, St Andrew's Street ('Barrestrete'), Winnetts Lane, Tower Hill, Ricketts Lane (Bagbridge Street) and Queen Street (Goseford Street).

Friar Street's tannery existed in the 11th and 12th centuries, and there is evidence at this time that the east end of Friar Street had a (late Saxon) road, lying to the north of the present street. The ditch to the north of this road was filled in, possibly to allow the construction of a building before 1200; soil on top of the Saxon road may show that it remained in use as a trackway. From the 13th century, after the charter was granted, Friar Street developed into a desirable residential area, with a new cobbled road pre-dating the fire, again to the north of the present street. At the west end the tannery makes way for a 12th- or 13th-century timber-framed house, later partly destroyed by a fire. By the early 14th century a new timber-framed building with a tiled roof was constructed on the site; in the 16th century more redevelopment occurred, with two substantial sandstone and timber-framed buildings erected. In the 14th century a house was built at the east end of Friar Street; Chorley House, further along, was a fine, large late 14th-century timber-framed building, demolished in 1962 (the car park site on the north of Friar Street); Steynor's Court towards the west end was probably a 16th-century timber-framed house, demolished around 1900; and Priory House, still standing at the west end, dates from the 15th to 17th centuries. By 1500, therefore, Friar Street was a wealthy residential area, although not very far from the Great Pit and the salt industry.

In addition to the main town streets, Winnetts Lane and Vines Lane had medieval buildings fronting onto them. Queen Street and Hanbury Street were probably built up on both sides, as the 17th-century map shows (*see* frontispiece).

The churches are all apparently medieval, as shown by both documentary evidence and their surviving fabric. The parish boundaries divide the town centre in an interesting way, as shown on the 17th-century map.

St Andrew's may be a remnant of an early Saxon minster, as Domesday Book indicates its pre-Conquest existence; or, it is possible that it was a daughter-chapel of St Mary's. The present church dates from the early 13th century, with rebuilding after the fire from the early 14th century and later. It is in a very cramped position for the main parish church of the town, suggesting either that it may have been fitted in to an existing layout, and thus post-dates the establishment of streets and buildings in that part of the town, or that its status, when built, was not that of a minster or parish church.

St Mary-next-Witton is first recorded in 1200, the church for one of the two manors at Witton. By 1349 it was in bad repair, possibly indicating shifting or shrinkage of the settlement; it had 'not 10 inhabitants' in 1427-8 and was later demolished. The parish united with St Andrew's in 1662. Its site survives as St Andrew's and St Mary's churchyard, between Highfield Hospital and the *Castle Hotel*.

St Peter-de-Witton is the church for the other Witton manor, dating from the early 12th century; its stained glass includes 13th- and 14th-century pieces. Next to the manor house, it was probably at the nucleus of the agricultural settlement; its parish took in part of High Street, Hanbury Street, Queen Street and Chapel Bridge, named after a dependent chapel of St Peter's which, sited on the bridge, actually had the road running through it. This extraordinary structure, built (or rebuilt) in the early 1500s, was demolished in 1763.

St Nicholas' church existed at the junction of Friar Street and Winnetts Lane. A chapel-of-ease originally, in 1170 it was given to the Cistercian nuns at Westwood. Having been damaged or destroyed in the fire, in 1291 it became a rectory and served as the parish church for the west of the town. After the Dissolution it passed with Westwood to the Pakington family, and the 14th-century stone grave-cover, incorporated in a 16th-century chimney in Friar Street, was probably removed from the church at that time. During the Civil War it was ruined, but the ruins were not cleared completely until the 19th century, and some windows and gargoyles were incorporated into the *Old Cock Inn* further along Friar Street.

St Augustine's on Dodderhill is not a Droitwich church, but rather the parish church for Dodderhill whose population centre is Wychbold. It dominates Droitwich, standing on the Roman fort site; with its originally cruciform plan, it may have been a Saxon church, although its surviving fabric agrees with the documented date of 1178 for its foundation. It suffered damage in the Civil War—hence its rather odd plan now.

Other religious foundations existed: in 1285 the rector of Dodderhill founded the Hospital of St Mary, north of Chapel Bridge, thought to be a hostel for travellers and/or a poorhouse; it was suppressed in 1535-6. An Augustinian Friary was founded in the Vines area in 1331, and extended in 1343 and 1351; by 1531 it was in a decayed state, with only one friar.

The Civil War resulted in some destruction of salt-making equipment, and the damage to three of the churches. The salt industry appears to have continued, however, and schemes to transport the salt by water were put forward from the mid-17th century onwards.

Post-Monopoly and Spa Town

The end of the borough's monopoly on salt production led to a major change in the economic status quo; many individuals and institutions whose wealth derived from a share in the old brine pits were ruined, and many new owners of brine wells became rich very quickly. This is reflected in the town, with much re-facing in brick of timber-framed buildings, and new Georgian and Victorian (18th- and 19th-century) brick buildings. Among these is the Town Hall, built in 1826 to replace the demolished Exchequer House; the 16th-century heraldic glass from the latter was moved to St Andrew's manor house, now the central part of the *Raven Hotel*.

Previously impassable roads were turnpiked, that is, tolls were charged to pay for surfacing and maintenance; in 1713 the Chapel Bridge to Worcester road was the first in the county to be turnpiked, followed in 1749 by Chapel Bridge to Bromsgrove and Hanbury Road to Bradley Brook. The canal built in 1768-71 improved transportation still further.

The 19th century saw the construction of large salt works in the Vines and Covercroft, with subsequent pollution; in the Vines and at the west end of Friar Street, tenements were thrown up to house the new workers. The canal was extended in 1852; in the same year the railway reached Droitwich. This heyday of salt production was short-lived, and the industry moved to Stoke Prior towards the end of the century.

During a cholera epidemic in 1832, sufferers were immersed in warm brine (hot baths being a recommended treatment); various ailments were almost miraculously alleviated. Dr. Ricketts' 'asylum' (hospital) dates from this time; it still exists in Friar Street (Droitwich Working Men's Club and the building to the west). Dr. William Bainbrigge was involved in the construction of the first brine baths, situated in Queen Street (the Royal Brine Baths). The spa expanded as the salt industry declined, with John Corbett a major influence in both spheres, determined to change the image of Droitwich as a dirty industrial town. He built the St Andrew's Brine Baths in 1887, enlarged and converted St Andrew's House to the *Raven Hotel* in the same year, and built the Salters' Hall in Victoria Square for concerts and public meetings. He built the *Worcestershire Hotel* in 1891, smaller then than now, and the *Park Hotel* (now the *Herriotts*); the Lido Park (originally the Brine Baths Park) was laid out and St John's Hospital provided for the treatment of the poor; and he gave land and money for the new railway station, opened in 1899.

This was the time when spas were fashionable, and Droitwich Spa was different in that it treated illness as well as providing rest and recreation. Numerous other hotels and boarding houses sprang up and, after the First World War, Highfield House was converted to a hospital and began treating soldiers, and later on treated less affluent patients from the Birmingham area. The Spa industry declined gradually from the 1920s, and St Andrew's Brine Baths closed in 1970; the new Brine Baths Hospital continues the tradition of using brine for medical purposes, as does St John's Hospital.

The first housing estate was built at Newtown, off Ombersley Street, in the 1880s, and shortly after 1900 Corbett Avenue and Lyttelton Road were laid out, followed by other areas in Witton. Early this century there was little development south of Witton Hill, and nothing beyond Grantham Bridge on the Kidderminster side. The Everton brothers began development to the west and east of Worcester Road in the 1920s and '30s. The Vines area, a notorious slum, was cleared in the 1930s and the Park was laid out, including St Richard's statue; although at that time the location of the Upwich Pit had been lost, the statue is in fact fairly close to the pit!

The town retained its old plan, central parts of which may date from Saxon and medieval times, until the 1970s when the Saltway and the shopping precinct altered the street layout and resulted in the removal of many older buildings. High Street, a commercial centre for centuries, has become virtually deserted. (Interestingly, High Street was almost level up to about 1910: because the brine stream runs under High Street, pumping of brine at the Stoke Prior salt works resulted in pronounced subsidence and in the leaning buildings visible today.)

Surviving Buildings of Interest

Timber-framed buildings, 13th-17th centuries:

31 High Street is probably the oldest domestic building in Droitwich, a 14th-century town house set at right angles to the street, originally jettied at first-floor level, with a side passage at the east; a four-bay great chamber and two-bay antechamber lie behind. The street frontage is mid-18th-century brickwork, probably with timber framing behind it at first-floor level.

Similarly, the following are all timber-framed buildings re-faced in brick: 15 (east part) & 17 High Street, 16th-century; 33-35 High Street, late 17th-century; 40 Friar Street, the

Hop Pole Inn, 17th century; and possibly 14 & 16 and 30 High Street, and 56 and 58 Friar Street.

Buildings which retain their timber-framed appearance include 21-23 High Street, 17th-century but recently much altered; 20 & 22 High Street, 17th-century; 44 & 46 High Street, Bullocks, 16th-century; 21 Queen Street, 16th-century; 36-38 Friar Street, Priory House, 15th-17th centuries; 79 Friar Street, 15th- or 16th-century; 27 Bromsgrove Road, 16th-century; *Raven Hotel*, former St Andrew's manor house, 17th-century; St Peter's Manor, 1618, and Barns, 16th-17th centuries with modern restoration; Chawson farmhouse, 16th-17th century; and Boycott farmhouse, with 16th-century rear wing.

In 1990, 5-7 Queen Street was demolished; this was one of the oldest surviving buildings, with a 15th-century timber-framed rear wing and 17th-century timber-framed street frontage block, the latter re-faced in brick during the 18th century. The adjoining 9 Queen Street, the *Royal Exchange Hotel*, was also demolished because it was thought dangerous, but should be reconstructed eventually; originally 17th-century, this timber-framed building was either a merchant's house or a first-floor market hall on timber posts, with the ground-floor area open (hence the staircase tower, to give access to the upper chamber).

Brick buildings, 17th-19th centuries:

The Coventry almshouses in the Holloway, although much altered now, date from the 17th century and result from a wager between Sir John Pakington of Westwood and Sir Henry Coventry of Croome Court; the former lost, and paid for almshouses named after the winner (who also contributed to the cost of finishing the buildings).

The south side, west end of the High Street is mid-18th-century Georgian new building, like 27-29 (Tenby House) across the street. Friar Street has many new 18th- and 19th-century buildings on both sides, including the *Old Cock Inn*, built (or rebuilt) early in the 19th century by an 'antiquarian' builder who re-used features from old St Nicholas' church, then ruined.

At the corner of The Holloway and Hanbury Street stands a mid-18th-century tollhouse, which has recently been altered.

Conclusion

Droitwich and its heritage is unique, in regional, national and international contexts. It is hoped that this brief account will enable the people who live and work in the town, and all who are interested in Droitwich, to understand its past, know about what remains from earlier centuries, and support or join in with work to preserve this heritage.

LYN BLEWITT
September 1994

Old Maps

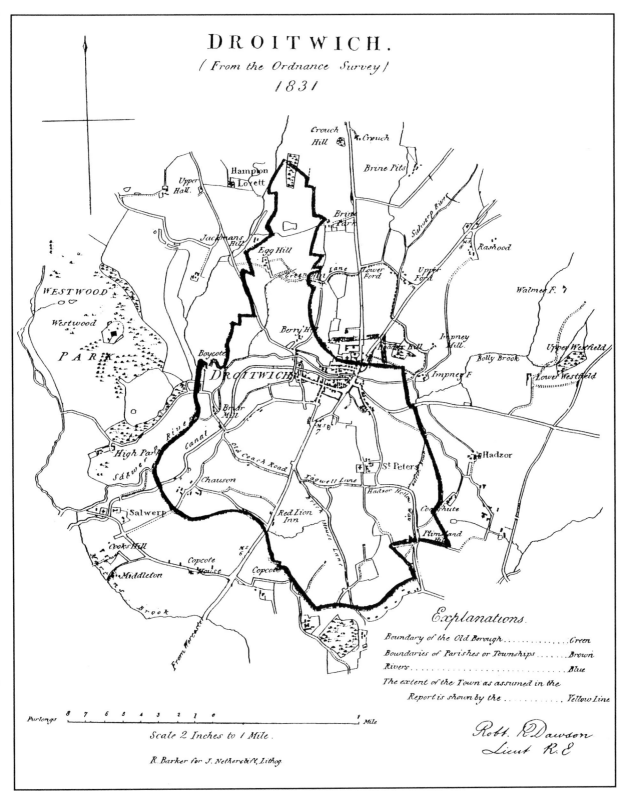

1. Map of Droitwich parish, 1831.

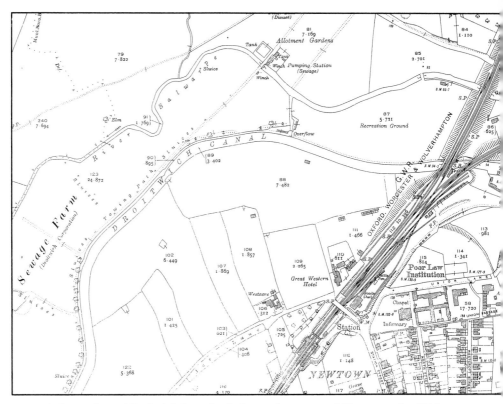

2. Street plans of Droitwich from the Ordnance Survey map 25" to one mile, 1938.

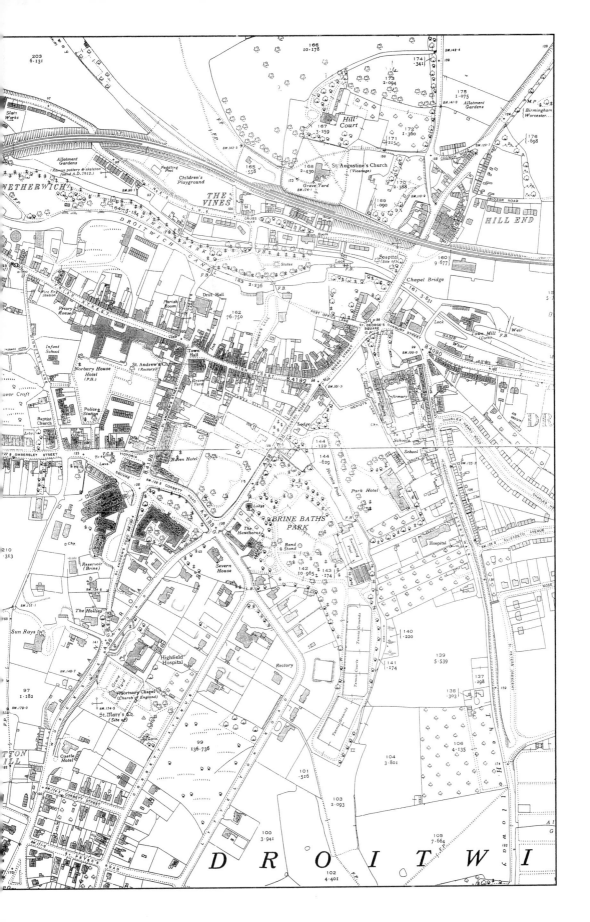

Streets & Buildings

3. High Street, looking west from Queen Street, *c.*1860. You will see that the road is level, unlike today. St Andrew's church can be seen at the far end.

4. The *Talbot Inn*, High Street, *c.*1880. A 1650-1700 two-storey timber-framed building originally, a brick façade and a third storey were added in the 18th/19th century with a rear range rebuilt 1830-40. The front was recently completely rebuilt.

5. Another view of High Street looking west from Queen Street, *c*.1900. Bolton's grocery shop can be seen on the right.

6. Swains' stationer's shop, on the corner of High Street and Tower Hill, *c*.1890. This was a 1740-50 red-brick painted building which was given a Grade II listing. It became Bolton's grocery shop in 1960, but is now unoccupied.

7. On the other side of Tower Hill are two more old buildings. They were also 1740-50 red brick buildings (again Grade II listed) and the first now has a Victorian shop-front. In 1953 it was occupied by Brewster's outfitters and is now the home of High Park Antiques. The second was a private residence (with political poster in the windows) and now houses a florist and a business bureau.

8. George Wythes grocery shop located at the east end of High Street in 1900. Many people will remember the premises being occupied by Doug Miles' cycle shop. It now houses Swinton Insurance Co.

9. High Street, looking east towards Queen Street in 1908. Gurney's Lane can be seen on the left just past the *Crown Inn* (no longer there) and the boots hanging outside Harney's bootmakers.

10. Mid-summer floods in High Street during the First World War. The road now dips due to subsidence caused by the underlying salt streams. George Baylis' butchers is on the right.

11. More serious floods at the eastern end of High Street in 1924. Floods of 18 inches deep were experienced several times a year. Major flooding—reaching a depth of six feet—occurred twice in 50 years, the last time in January 1963. Improved drainage has since cured the problem.

12. Rear view of 17 High Street taken in 1953. This has an early 19th-century front concealing a 16th-century timber-framed structure and, together with the east part of the adjoining building (no. 15), was a 1580s jettied timber-framed building with brick front added late in the 18th century. To the rear is a timber-framed range dating from 1650-60 and recently restored. The shop fronts are Victorian.

13. Queen Street *c*.1850, and the *Royal Exchange Hotel* (on the left). This hotel was listed in 1980 as a Grade II building as it was dated 17th-19th centuries with a 16th-century staircase tower. It was possibly a merchant's mansion, or a market hall built *c*.1628 as a first-floor chamber supported on posts over an open ground-floor area, with a staircase providing access to the chamber. When adjoining buildings were demolished in 1989/90, it was considered structurally unsafe and quickly demolished in March 1990. It is due to be reconstructed in its original form, but a lot of the original materials have been lost.

14. Cottage adjoining the *Red Lion Inn* in Queen Street, *c*.1895. (Now an Indian restaurant.) This is a late 16th-century timber-framed building, originally extending further to the north and now with only two bays remaining. The windows and door-case were added in the 18th and 19th centuries.

15. The shop of T. F. Cooke, Meat Purveyor, in Queen Street, *c*.1900. Thomas Francis Cooke sold his land and buildings to the Salt Union for £580 in 1889 when they were buying up all the land in that area. The premises are now occupied by Levett and Hill and the shopfront is inscribed 'Established 1859'.

16. *Red Lion Inn*, Queen Street, *c*.1900. This building was once part of the adjoining one—see illustration 14. There is now an empty shop on this site.

17. Laying the pipes in Queen Street that would carry the brine from the brine pits in the Vines to the Brine Baths, 1903. The foreman's name is Causier, this being an old Droitwich name which appears in St Peter's church parish register in 1713. Thomas Causier owned land in Gurney's Lane, occupied by a salt works, which he sold to the Salt Union in 1864/65.

18. The east side of Queen Street in 1906. The premises of Charles Jones Skerrett, tobacconist, and Mrs. M. Smith, a local printer and stationer who ran the *Guardian* office, can be seen.

19. Another view of the east side of Queen Street, just past Herriotts Lane, and outside Harber's shop, a dyers, *c*.1910. The road is being re-surfaced.

20. Queen Street, showing the *Royal Exchange Hotel* in 1918. The dyer's notice on the other side of the road is still there, but the adjoining premises have disappeared.

21. Floods in Queen Street seen from St George's Square in 1924. The *Red Lion Inn* is on the right.

22. A view of St George's Square and Queen Street from Chapel Bridge in 1918. The building on the left is now a furniture shop and the old *St George's Hotel* is behind the trees. Notice how tall the telegraph poles were at that time.

23. Queen Street, looking north, in August 1937 with the *Royal Exchange Hotel* on the left. None of the buildings on the right are there today as they were demolished to make way for road widening in 1951.

24. The Worcester-Birmingham road (A38) near The Herriotts, prior to widening in 1951.

25. The road widening of the Worcester-Birmingham road in progress, 1951.

26. Coronation celebrations for King George V in 1911 outside Mr. C. Freeman's house in Friar Street. This house became a Picture Palace—'The Silver Pix'.

27. The town's first cinema on the north-east side of Friar Street. This picture was taken in 1953. The building was demolished in 1962.

28. Friar Street in 1918. The *Old Cock Inn* is on the right and Priory House is in the distance on the left.

29. Friar Street, looking west in 1953 and showing houses which were demolished in 1962. There was much evidence in Friar Street that it was a well organised salt production centre in the second and third century B.C.

30. Nos. 21 and 23 Friar Street in 1953, also demolished in 1962. These were opposite the bottom of Winnetts Lane.

31. The adjoining premises, Nos. 27 and 29 Friar Street in 1953. Again, they were demolished in 1962.

32. Nos. 56 to 64 Friar Street in 1953. Nos. 56 and 58, which are the two right-hand buildings, are of the 18th century, although a timber truss in the west gable of No. 56 may suggest refaced or partially rebuilt timber-framed houses. Nos. 60/62—now Ladbrookes—was originally a timber-framed building dating from the late 14th/early15th century with a 17th century chimney-stack remaining. It was refaced or rebuilt in the 18th century and the windows are 19th-century. No. 64 is an early 19th-century brick building. All these houses are listed as Grade II buildings.

33. Friar Street, looking east in 1953. In the right-hand foreground is the *Hop Pole Inn*, a timber-framed building of the 1600s, refaced in the early 1700s with brick and still in a good condition.

34. Gable House, Friar Street in 1954—another demolished timber-framed building.

35. Chorley House, a 14th-century timber-framed building in Friar Street in 1960. Despite being listed in 1951 as a Grade II building, it was demolished in 1962.

36. No. 89 Friar Street (Chorley House), just before its demolition in 1962. It appears that this street had a number of town houses in the 13th century and was then the 'upmarket' part of the town.

37. Another view of Chorley House just before it was demolished in 1962. The council claimed that it did not have sufficient funds to restore it.

38. Rear of 85, 87 and 89 Friar Street with Norbury House in the background, 1960. These labourers' cottages were demolished soon afterwards. In the last century, the street contained the homes of many labourers and salt workers due to its proximity to the salt works in the Vines.

39. A view of Victoria Square in 1890 showing Salters' Hall and the *Raven Hotel*.

40. Victoria Square in 1910, looking east. The trees in the centre have been replaced by a paved area. The town war memorial is situated here.

41. Four-in-hand coach outside Salters' Hall in Victoria Square. St Andrew's Brine Baths is in the background.

42. The stables in Victoria Square in 1910. They were once opposite the *Raven Hotel*.

43. Victoria Square again in 1910, with Salters' Hall on the right.

44. Ombersley Street in 1918, looking towards Victoria Square. The Covercroft salt works, which lay behind the wooden fencing on the left, was no longer operating.

45. The junction of Ombersley Street and Victoria Square in 1953. The war memorial can now be seen.

46. The junction of Winnetts Lane and Ombersley Street in 1920. The pharmacy on the corner was bought by Boots and the whole of this site is now occupied by Barclays Bank.

WORCESTER ROAD DROITWICH.

47. Worcester Road at the junction of St Andrew's Road (on the left), looking from Witton Hill in 1900. The house has gone and a roundabout now occupies the site.

48. Worcester Road in 1905, showing the entrance to Brine Baths Park. The poster shows that the Irish Guards band were playing there.

49. An engraving showing Chapel Bridge in 1833. The old chapel, demolished in 1763, stood where the house stands on the south side of the bridge, but straddling the bridge, and the main road passed through the middle of it. Dr. Treadway Nash, vicar of St Peter's church (1761-91), in his book *Worcestershire*, describes the location as 'through the middle of the Chapel passed the high road leading to Bromsgrove, the reading desk and pulpit being on one side of the road and the congregation sitting on the other'.

50. A painting by John Cotton in 1875 of Chapel Bridge and the adjoining house. Dodderhill church is in the background.

51. The last thatched cottage in Droitwich. This was in Vines Lane in 1905. In 1986 it was discovered that a late Roman or early post-Roman cemetery containing 14 burials lay underneath this road. It may have been part of a larger burial ground.

52. The Vines in 1910. This was an area of vineyards in Roman times, but early this century it was considered to be a slum area containing salt workers' cottages. Some years later, the houses were demolished and Vines Park was laid out. Dodderhill church is in the background.

53. The Holloway (originally Hollow Way), *c*.1890. The cottages on the left were built on the site of the original St John's Hospital.

54. The Holloway in 1900—then just a peaceful country lane!

55. The Holloway in 1910, but now under development with houses being built on the east side. The west side which largely contained the borders of St Peter's Fields remained and still remains undeveloped today.

56. St Andrew's Manor House in 1870, a late 16th-century building with 18th-century and later additions. The central part is a 16th/17th-century timber-framed building with 18th-century windows and porch. It became the *Raven Hotel*, owned by John Corbett, and has since been further extended.

57. Randolph House, St Andrew's Street dates from the mid-18th century and incorporates timber framing from an earlier building. This is now the Spinning Wheel restaurant.

58. Hanbury Street (now Hanbury Road) in 1937. The *Barley Mow Inn* is on the right.

59. Another view of Hanbury Street (south side) in 1937 at its junction with Holloway. The buildings have long gone.

60. Witton Hill, *c*.1900, the main road out of Droitwich southward to Worcester.

61. Woodfield Road in 1903, with the entrance to Bradley's salt works and Chapel Bridge salt works.

62. Old Coach Road in 1910 with Witton Pool on the corner, taken from the Worcester Road. A group of houses built by John Corbett, with the raven crest on them, can be seen.

63. Grantham Bridge straddling the Kidderminster Road in 1937.

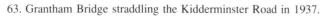

64. Tower Hill in 1953, looking south. The outside wall of the Brine Baths pumping station is in the right foreground.

65. The Drill Hall which was situated in Ricketts Lane in 1953.

66. Post Office Lane looking
south towards the west end
of the High Street in 1953.
The lane is no longer there
following the construction
of the inner ring road
(Saltway).

67. Winnetts Lane, looking
north from the main school
in the town, 1953. There is
now a large car park on this
site serving St Andrew's
shopping precinct.

68. Winnetts Lane looking north, taken near the Police Station in 1953. At that time, the police operated from a converted house.

69. Winnetts Lane looking north-east, taken from opposite the school in 1953. Dodderhill church is on the hill in the background and Norbury House on the right.

70. Church Road, Dodderhill in 1953. This road, as the name implies, leads up the hill to Dodderhill church.

71. Print of St Andrew's church and Town Hall in 1851. The Town Hall was built in 1825 superceding the Exchequer building. The ground floor was open and used for the weekly market. The town stocks were in the square in front of the building.

72. St Andrew's church in 1911 with an adjoining house (now the Parish Room). The main part of the church dates from 1290, but there are earlier fragments in its structure. The tower was reduced in height in 1828 as subsidence had made it dangerous. Inside the church is a memorial tablet to Captain Norbury who fought alongside Admiral Benbow in the West Indies.

73. Another picture of the house next to St Andrew's church, taken in 1953. This was originally the vestry for St Andrew's church. It was a late 17th-/early 18th-century two-storey brick house with a rear wing probably built in the 19th century, and again in brick, but using 14th- or 15th-century moulded beams. These are likely to have come from the south aisle of the church which was restored at that time. The house was totally demolished in 1980 and rebuilt using different materials.

74. The rebuilding and strengthening of St Andrew's church tower in 1911, following the reduction in height carried out in 1828.

75. Print of the old St Nicholas church tower in 1825. This church was built of stone by the Nuns of Westwood early in the 14th century, and remained in their possession until the Dissolution of the Smaller Monasteries in 1536. It is probable that Henry VIII either gave or sold the estates of the priory of Westwood to Sir John Pakington and he had the right in 1542 of presenting a clerk to the living. For the next one hundred years the church and rectory went with Hampton Lovett manor, the seat of the Pakingtons. It was in ruins by the end of the Civil War (1651) during which time soldiers had been billeted in it. The tower remained and was eventually demolished in about 1830. A window from the church dating from about 1320 can be seen in the *Old Cock Inn* in Friar Street.

76. St Peter's church in 1857. The earliest parts of this church are a Norman chancel with three small windows, and a Norman chancel arch. There are also traces of 13th-century structures and some early 14th-century windows. Inside the church is an imposing monument to George Wylde, 1616, who was Lord Chief Baron of the Exchequer under Thomas Cromwell. In the nave there is a modern tablet to Edward Winslow, who was one of the Pilgrim Fathers who sailed to America in the *Mayflower* in 1620. He was baptised in the church in 1595, and many Americans visit Droitwich to see his memorial.

77. An 1833 engraving showing the Coventry Almshouses in The Holloway. They were built in the latter part of the 17th century. A school was included for 40 boys and 40 girls of the borough, which survived until the establishment of free education in the late 1890s.

78. Coventry Almshouses in 1953. Five new almshouses were built at the rear in 1902 from additional income available after the hospital school was closed.

79. The *George Inn* and *Royal Hotel* in St George's Square in 1875. They were built in 1836 next to the first brine baths (the Royal Brine Baths) in Droitwich. They were all demolished in about 1900.

80. The Herriotts, 1860. It was enlarged to become the *Park Hotel* in the 1890s and later reverted to its original name and became an old peoples' home.

81. Buildings on the east side of Worcester Road being demolished in 1951 as part of the road widening. Part of a human skeleton was unearthed from one of the houses on 2 March 1912.

82. Herriott's Cottage, seen from the corner of High Street in 1953.

83. The Town Hall (built in 1825) at the junction of St Andrew's Street and Friar Street in 1900.

84. Bays Meadow cottage in 1885. The building is still there but is derelict. It was in this part of Droitwich that the remains of a Roman villa were discovered during the excavations of 1847, with further evidence in 1926/7. A second Roman building on this site was excavated in 1954/5. It proved to be a substantial second-century villa with 18 rooms and several finds denoting that the owner was wealthy and possibly an imperial administrator or entrepreneur controlling the production of salt. There has been subsequent work by Birmingham University from 1967 onwards. Worked flint tools have been found in the excavations possibly dating from the Mesolithic period.

85. The original railway station, c.1890. It was built in 1852 when the railway (Oxford/Wolverhampton line) first reached the town.

86. Demolition of salt workers' cottages by Vines Park in 1900. A large number of similar cottages were built in the town in the 19th century.

87. Priory House, Friar Street, restored in the 1970s by the Droitwich Preservation Trust. This house was largely refurbished in the 17th century but there is a solar wing dating back to about 1500.

88. 'Ye Olde Curiosity
Shoppe' in 1900, on the site
of the *Barley Mow*, Hanbury
Road. The proprietor was
C. F. Bullock.

89. 'Ye Olde Curiosity Shoppe'—a different one—in 1900. This one was Raven Cottage, Hill End, built in
1878 as a Corbett estate cottage and bearing an heraldic panel with the Corbett raven emblem. The
building is still there and is a private house.

90. St. John's Hospital, The Holloway in 1910. Built by John Corbett for the 'working class'. It was administered by trustees and for many years the chairman was Mr. Dyson Perrins of Worcestershire Sauce fame. It was a subscription hospital, i.e. tickets were issued to subscribers which could be handed to deserving cases.

91. *Old Cock Inn*, Friar Street in 1910, it was first licensed in 1712 in the reign of Queen Anne and incorporates windows taken from the original St Nicholas church. It is reputed to have been the scene of Judge Jeffries infamous Assizes. One of the carvings on the wall, said to be of the judge, has a frog coming out of its mouth.

92. The original *Barley Mow*, Hanbury Street, 1910. It has been replaced by a more modern building, but still bears the same name.

93. *Great Western Hotel* near the station in 1918, long since gone. The site has been used for light industry.

94. Interior of Salters' Hall, Victoria Square in 1920. This building was the hub of society with dances, bazaars and theatrical shows taking place there.

95. Exterior of Salters' Hall, Victoria Square in 1920. It was built by John Corbett as a recreation place for his work people. The hall remained the property of the Corbett Trustees until sold to Mr. Charles Henry Everton in the early 1930s. It later became Salters Super Cinema and is now the public library which still contains the proscenium arch and gallery of the cinema.

96. Salters' Hall and *Raven Hotel* in 1930. The *Raven Hotel* was originally St Andrew's House and was converted into a hotel by John Corbett in 1887. It is the reputed birthplace of St Richard de Wyche, later Bishop of Chichester.

97. The Winter Gardens, 1952. They were finally demolished in the 1980s and a private hospital, including brine baths, is now on the site.

98. Portion of the timbered roof in St Peter's Manor House, taken in 1953. The house is thought to have been erected in 1618 and restored in 1867. It was the former seat of the Nash family.

99. An inscription over the fireplace in St Peter's Manor House, also taken in 1953.

100. Union Lane Chapel in 1953 (since demolished). This was the chapel for the workhouse.

101. Boycott Farm in 1956. It was listed as a 1700s building with a 1500s rear wing and originally was probably a 15th- or 16th-century timber-framed building. It was converted in 1973/4 to flats when many original features were lost and poor quality workmanship was used. It has not been well maintained since and was recently under threat of demolition. However, following many objections, it has been saved and is at present unoccupied.

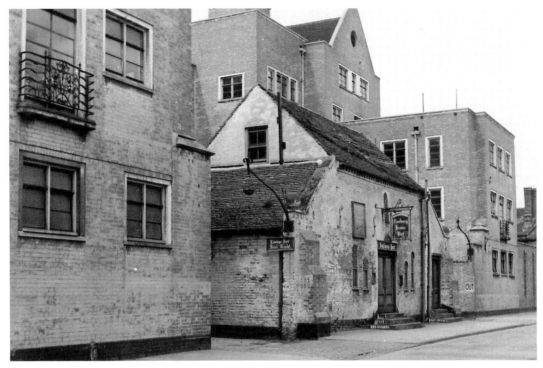

102. *Norbury House Bar*, Friar Street in 1960, since demolished. *Norbury House Hotel* was built around this building in the 1930s and was one of the leading Midland hotels. It had an entrance in Victoria Square with a walkway through attractive gardens. In 1939, it was requisitioned by the War Department and used for billeting troops. After the war, it was converted into flats and later housed the Town Council and many of its departments. It has now been reconverted into flats and accommodates the town's theatre.

103. Three black and white half-timbered houses opposite Winnetts Lane in 1958.

Salt Industry

104. The Vines salt works in 1860. Passengers on the railway, which ran above this area, used to complain that they could not see the town because of the smoke from the chimneys.

105. A building in the Vines salt works, 1912. These works were owned by the Fardon family, Jonathan Fardon having purchased them from Richard Nash of Worcester in 1824.

106. Cherry Orchard salt works, on the corner of Union Lane, in 1910.

107. Another view of the Cherry Orchard salt works taken in 1912. It belonged to the Old Droitwich Salt Co. in 1771 and stretched from Ricketts Lane to Winnetts Lane along the Vines.

108. A view of Cherry Orchard salt works from the canal side, taken about 1912-16.

109. Another view of Cherry Orchard salt works in 1912.

110. Staff and employees standing in front of a Manning Wardle locomotive outside the loading shed at the Covercroft salt works in 1897.

111. A view of Covercroft salt works in Ombersley Street, 1899. On this site now is the old library, shops and offices.

112. A section of the dryer room in Covercroft salt works in 1900. The temperature was kept at 300 degrees Fahrenheit. The salt was only kept here for 12 hours.

113. The drying pans in Covercroft salt works receiving attention from two salt workers, 1900.

114. The furnaces, which were houses beneath the salt drying pans, receiving attention. Covercroft salt works, 1900.

115. Another view of the furnaces in Covercroft salt works, 1900.

116. Railway lines for conveying salt from the Covercroft salt works, 1910.

117. A group of salt packers in Covercroft salt works taken in 1910.

118. Two female salt packers in
Covercroft salt works in 1910.

119. Stoking up in the salt works,
c.1910. Most workers (even the women
in earlier years) were stripped to the
waist because of the heat.

120. The entrance to Covercroft salt works off Ombersley Street. The locomotive was built by Manning Wardle in 1878 in Leeds. The engine driver is J. (Ike) Pugh and the salt loaders are John Simpson, Elias Colley, William Colley and James Harris (foreman).

121. The entrance to the Chapel Bridge salt works on the Worcester-Birmingham road in 1899. In the background is a heap of salt pickings from the salt pans, which is salt burnt hard on the bottom of the pan owing to excessive heat. The salt maker removed it with special hammers once a week. The timber construction is the brine reservoir or brine tun which supplies the whole of the salt pans. Brine was pumped from brine pits at the bottom of Post Office Lane near the canal and piped to these works. The water supplied for cleaning and washing the salt tubs was conveyed from Herriott's Pool by pipe line along Queen Street and over Chapel Bridge.

122. Chapel Bridge salt works in 1900. The works contained six fine salt pans and four broad salt pans together with the grind salt mill.

123. The railway sidings for Chapel Bridge salt works, the chimneys of which can be seen on the left, in 1911. In the right background is Dodderhill church. Also on the left is the old tower of St Andrew's church, the old Town Mills and the rear elevation of the *Barley Mow Inn*. The railway siding running down to the salt works was called Clay Sideway after one of the original owners of the salt works. It started as Clay and Newman Salt Works before the time of the old Droitwich Salt Co. when Mr. John Bradley was manager. He built Oaklands and was mayor of Droitwich. The chimney stack just visible in the extreme background, and above the railway lines, was the property of Joseph Ashby Fardon, who owned the salt works in the Vines. He was also a mayor of Droitwich.

124. Chapel Bridge salt works
being demolished in 1911.

125. Chapel Bridge salt works
derelict in 1912. Dodderhill
church can be seen in the
background and Droitwich
Canal in the foreground.

126. Bradleys salt works in Hanbury Road, which became Everton's garage. The building is in front of the Town Mill, prior to its catching fire in 1909. The steam engine was used for hauling stone for the roads.

127. Friar Street salt works in 1912.

128. Pumping station near the canal in Post Office Lane, 1900. Steam engines were introduced in the 18th century to pump brine from the pits.

129. The Salt Union shop in 1900, which stood at the end of High Street, and the rear of the premises in Ricketts Lane—originally Bagbridge Lane and then Back Bridge Lane. It was replaced by a building used by the Co-op butchers and grocers and is now a carpet shop.

130. The interior of the Salt Union shop, 1900. The Salt Union was formed in 1889 as an amalgamation of numerous small salt companies.

131. St Andrew's Brine Baths, soon after they were built by John Corbett in 1887. The original Royal Brine Baths, together with the *Royal Hotel*, were erected on the east side of Queen Street in 1836 and demolished in *c*.1900 (*see* illustration 79). The curative properties of brine were discovered during the great cholera epidemic of 1832.

132. Members of staff of the Royal Brine Baths, 1899.

133. Another view of the Brine Baths in 1902. People came from all over the country to use the baths which caused a rapid growth in the hotel and boarding house business as well as the opening of many private hospitals.

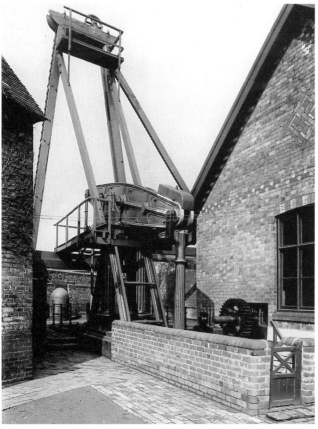

134. Brine Baths pump situated behind Tower Hill, 1910.

135. The Brine Baths in 1953.

136. The chief engineer, Mr. William Bourne, with the salt deposits in the subterranean chamber beneath the Brine Baths in 1951.

People, Places and Events

137. A 1750 engraving showing a view of Droitwich from Dodderhill church. You can see some of the damage to the church caused by the Civil War.

138. An illustrated bill-head of J. Allen's hosiery shop showing the shop and the adjoining St Andrew's church, 1850.

THE DROITWICH SALINE BATHS.

The Droitwich Saline Waters are the most prompt and efficacious remedy for Gout, Rheumatism, Sciatica, Neurology, Scrofula, all Skin Diseases, and Spinal affections. Thousands of Invalids have availed themselves of this wonderful natural remedy. The number of Visitors have increased this season upwards of 500 per cent.!

The strength of these Waters is upwards of twelve times that of the waters of the ocean!!! They are fully saturated with salt, and are found 200 feet below the surface of the earth.

The Baths were established in the spring of 1836, and have since that period progressively increased in the estimation of the public. In consequence of the increase of Visitors, the Directors have now been enabled to reduce their scale of charges to the most liberal footing, in order to prompt a generous public to bestow on the poor (for whom a Bath is specially provided) the curative blessing these waters offer,

CHARGES.—A Single Bath, 2s.; a Cold or Shower Bath, 1s. 6d.; Servants' Single Hot Bath, 1s. 6d.; Children under fourteen years of age, half-price.

A Yearly Subscription allowing the Subscriber twenty-one transferable Tickets, 21s. Tickets are issued by the Hon. Secretary.

N.B.—Without a Ticket no person can bathe.

A few recent Cases of complete Cure are here Inserted.

In gratitude for such benefit, these Gentlemen have kindly permitted reference to be made to them.

Mr. Green, Upton-on-Severn, Farmer, Sciatica.
Mr. Wallbank, Horsefair, Birmingham, Gentleman, Rheumatic Gout.
Mr. Bocknall, Horsefair, Birmingham, Innkeeper, Paralytic Stroke.
Mr. Munn, Warwick, Miller, &c., Rheumatic Gout.
Mr. Healy, Great King Street, Birmingham, Manufacturer of Jewellery, Chronic Rheumatism and Sciatica.
Mr. Unitt, Birmingham, Silversmith, Rheumatic.
Mr. Sheppard, Bull Street, Birmingham, Laceman, Rheumatic.
Mr. Husselbee, Birmingham, Coal Merchant, Sciatica.
Mr. Ashton, Birmingham, Rule Manufacturer, Rheumatic Gout.
Mr. Cope, Birmingham, Rule Manufacturer, Rheumatic.
Mr. Jones, Barbican, London, Gentlemen, a severe Spinal Affection.
Mr. Thorn, King William Street, London, Merchant, a severe Scorbutic Attack.

Mr. W. G. Gabb, *Honorary Secretary*.
James Kiterall, Esq., *Surgeon*.

139. An extract from *Lascelles Directory*, 1850, advertising the Droitwich Saline Baths.

140. A view of Droitwich in 1857 looking towards Dodderhill church which was dedicated in 1220. Evidence of a Roman fort, probably established between the years A.D. 47 and 70, has been found on the site. The present tower was built in the 18th century.

141. The opening of the St Andrew's Brine Baths extension by the mayor of Droitwich in 1860. The Baths were extended several times as the facilities became more widely known and brine bathing was advertised for a wide range of ailments, from rheumatism, through to skin rashes and nervous depression.

142. Copy of an excursion bill issued by the Midland Railway in 1881. The journey took over four hours and cost 14s. 6d. (73 pence) for a first-class ticket, 10s. 6d. (53 pence) for a second-class ticket, and the excursion was for six days!

NO CHANGE OF CARRIAGE. NO STOPPAGE AFTER BROMSGROVE.

TO THE PUBLIC.

THIS popular Excursion having met with a success not at all contemplated, after the powerful opposition offered to it by the Great Western Compy. has enabled me to extend my original intention of a limited number ; I therefore respectfully request those who intend patronising this Excursion to obtain their Tickets by Monday Evening.

WILLIAM PAINE.

Cheltenham, Saturday 10 p. m.

Midland Railway.

EXCURSION TO
LONDON and BACK

ALLOWING SIX CLEAR DAYS IN LONDON,

With the option of returning out Friday, the 11th, or Wednesday the 16th, leaving Euston Square about 5 o'clock, due notice will be given of the precise time,

Wednesday, July 9th, 1851,

Leaving GLOUCESTER at 7, CHELTENHAM 7 30, ASHCHURCH at 7 40, DEFFORD at 8, WORCESTER at 8 20, DROITWITCH 8 30, BROMSGROVE 8 47, BIRMINGHAM at 9 50 a.m.

Arriving at Euston Square 12 45 p. m.

This Train will afford an opportunity of attending the

Queen's Visit to Guildhall, Grand Procession, the Great Agricultural Show, the gathering of the Druids, Grand Review, Crystal Palace, &c. &c.

First Class 14s. 6d. Second 10s. 6d.

Children under 12 years of age half price.

TICKETS MAY BE HAD OF

Mr. PAINE, Printer, Cheltenham, Mr. J. MARSDEN, 46, High Street, Worcester. Mr. MAILLARD, Gloucester,
Mr. JENNER, Tewkesbury, Mr.   Droitwitch ;
and Mr.   Bromsgrove.

143. A group of Droitwich people in 1895. Reading from left to right, they are: (Standing) John Tombs, not known, Miss Ditmas, Henry C. Tombs, Mrs. J. Tombs, Dr. P. A. Roden, Mrs. Botfield (May McConnell).

(Seated) Mrs. McConnell, Mr. Samuel Tombs, Evelyn Tombs, Mrs. Tombs, Mrs. Dunford (cousin Sue), Mrs. Dixon (Ida Tombs).

144. The railway station decorated to celebrate its re-opening by Sir Frederick Godson on 10 June 1899. He was standing in for John Corbett who provided additional land and the money (£700) for the buildings which were on both the up and down platforms. On the south-bound side, there was a space for horse cabs and other vehicles from the hotels. The north-bound side had terraced formal gardens. The station staff wore navy uniforms with black braid on the collars and cuffs. The stationmaster wore a frock coat and a gold-braided hat. The station was totally demolished in the mid-1980s and replaced by a modern building.

145. Another picture of the re-opening of the railway station, 1899. A lunch was held in Salters' Hall for the important guests although John Corbett was absent due to a family bereavement. The town band played during the lunch and afterwards in the Brine Baths park. The guests inspected the park, the grounds of Chateau Impney (Corbett's home), the Brine Baths hospital, Westwood House and a salt works and they were then entertained to tea at the *Worcestershire Hotel* (also a Corbett building).

146. The bookstall on Droitwich Station in 1899. The only person identified is the boy on the right who is William Hughes of Madeley Road, Sparkhill, Birmingham.

147. Sail barges *Harriet*, *William* and *Volunteer* on Droitwich Canal near Vines Park in 1900. The Droitwich Canal Co. was launched with an authorised capital of £15,000 in £100 shares and the first shareholders' meeting was held in March 1768. Work began on 27 June 1768 but by March 1770 the capital had all been spent and it was decided to raise a further £6,600 by issuing more shares. The canal was built under the supervision of James Brindley and opened in 1771. Its purpose was to carry salt to the River Severn at Hawford.

148. The Salt Union barge *Henry* on the Droitwich Canal, Vines Park in 1900. The bargeman is Dandy Bourne. By this time, the canal's fortunes were declining and by 1906 revenue did not cover maintenance. Commercial traffic ceased on the canal in 1916 and it was finally abandoned in 1939. The Droitwich Canals Trust has been working for some years to reopen it.

149. The pump house at the bottom of Post Office Lane in 1910.

150. Coventry Almshouses inmates in their uniforms (black poke bonnet, black dress, white apron and shawl) in 1900. Miss Pugh, in the centre of the picture, was celebrating her 97th birthday.

151. A group of children from St Peter's school, The Holloway, who danced around the maypole in Brine Baths Park on May Day, 1900. At this time the schoolgirls of Droitwich chose a May Queen and crowned her with a wreath of flowers. A May Day parade was organised by the local Friendly Societies and headed by Robin Hood characters.

152. More May Day celebrations in the Brine Baths Park near Herriott's Pool, 1990.

153. The town band in Brine Baths Park, 1910. The band was provided by the Corbett Trustees and originally played in Salters' Hall in the mornings, and the park in the afternoons. The bandstand is still used for occasional Sunday afternoon concerts in the summer.

154. Witton Pool at the east end of Old Coach Road, at its junction with Worcester Road, in 1900. Old Coach Road follows the route of the old coach road to Westwood House, formerly a nunnery and later the home of the Pakington family. This area is now part of Witton Middle School's grounds and the pool is no longer to be seen.

155. Repairing the barge lock near Chapel Bridge in 1902. Droitwich Canal joined the Junction Canal near this point. The Junction Canal, linking the Droitwich Canal and the Birmingham and Worcester Canal, was opened in 1853. It was built because of competition from the railways for carrying salt and coal.

156. The putting green at *Worcestershire Brine Baths Hotel*, 1905. The hotel was built in 1891 by John Corbett (the salt king) at a cost of £51,000. A local builder had gone bankrupt leaving two houses partly built on the site and Corbett converted these houses in to a hotel. He had just been elected a Member of Parliament and persuaded the Countess of Dudley to open it. She was the wife of the Earl of Dudley, once the Governor of Australia and later Colonel of the Worcestershire Yeomanry in the early days of the First World War. They lived at nearby Witley Court. The hotel is now twice its original size.

157. Mr. Alec Smith, the Town Crier, at the beginning of his period of office which ran from 1905 to 1921. He died in 1930.

158. Two sea-going barges, *Henry* and *Moreland,* near the canal wharf in 1907. Priory House can be seen in the background.

159. The visit of Dr. Booth, founder of the Salvation Army, to their rally outside Salters' Hall in 1908. William Booth (1829-1912) was a missionary in the East End of London who had previously been a Methodist preacher. The name, Salvation Army, was adopted in 1878 and the mission organised on military lines.

160. A coach awaiting passengers outside St Andrew's Brine Baths in 1908.

161. The Town Mill, situated by Chapel Bridge, on fire in 1909. Dodderhill church can be seen in the background.

162. Proclamation of the accession to the throne of King George V, being read outside the Town Hall in 1910.

163. Election campaigners outside the committee rooms in 1910. Two of the people identified are Mrs. Shirley Jones and on the extreme right, Lord Cobham.

164. Election crowds outside the Town Hall in January 1910. The contest for the mid-Worcestershire seat was between Hon. John C. Lyttelton (Unionist) and Mr. Cecil Harmsworth (Liberal/Radical). The result was a victory for John Lyttelton who polled 5,078 votes to his opponent's 4,975, a majority of 103. This overturned a Radical majority in 1906 of 554 votes.

165. Election crowds outside the *Raven Hotel* in 1910. There were riots at this time and the Riot Act was read. As a result, 12 men appeared in court in February and were committed to the Assizes.

166. *Raven Hotel* decorated for May Day, 1920.

167. Conveyances for the Brine Bath's patients, 1910. These took the patients to and from their hotels and boarding houses to the brine baths.

168. The Flower Show at Brine Baths Park, 1910.

169. Canopied and open-top charabancs in 1910, belonging to Worcester Electric Traction Co. Ltd. The open vehicle is a Daimler No. FK 425 and the driver is Reg Dyer.

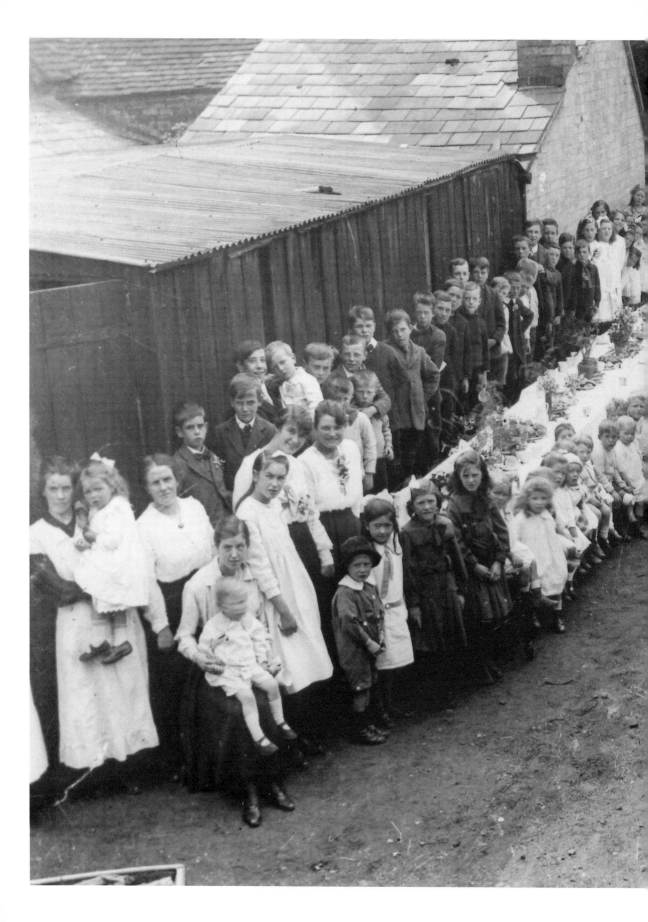

170. Street party celebrations for the coronation of King George V, 1910.

171. Official opening of the Brine Baths and Lido after their purchase by the Corporation from a private company, Droitwich Spa Ltd in 1954. Up to this time, an admission fee of one penny was charged. The picture shows Sir Claud Woodward speaking and the Hon. George Ward M.P. seated (arms folded).

172. A view of Droitwich looking south from the tower of Dodderhill church in 1953. The backs of the houses in the High Street can be seen.

173. Another view from Dodderhill church in 1953, looking west. Norbury House is clearly visible in the centre of the picture.

174. Aerial view of the centre of Droitwich in 1951. Victoria Square with Salters' Hall can be seen and also Winnetts Lane running off the bottom of the picture.